© 1999 Havoc Publishing

ISBN 1-57977-158-0

Published by Havoc Publishing
San Diego, California

Please write to us for more information

on Havoc Publishing products.

www.havocpub.com

Havoc Publishing

9808 Waples Street

San Diego, California 92121

Printed in Korea

THIS BOOK CELEBRATES THE MARRIAGE OF:

_____

&

_____

Contents

Contents

WILL YOU MARRY ME?

We will never forget the day of our proposal. We remember this story about that
special day _____

_____

_____

_____

_____

_____

_____

_____

_____

_____

_____

Our Engagement Announcement

I remember when we announced our engagement, we told_____
_____

Here are some of the first thoughts from our friends and family_____

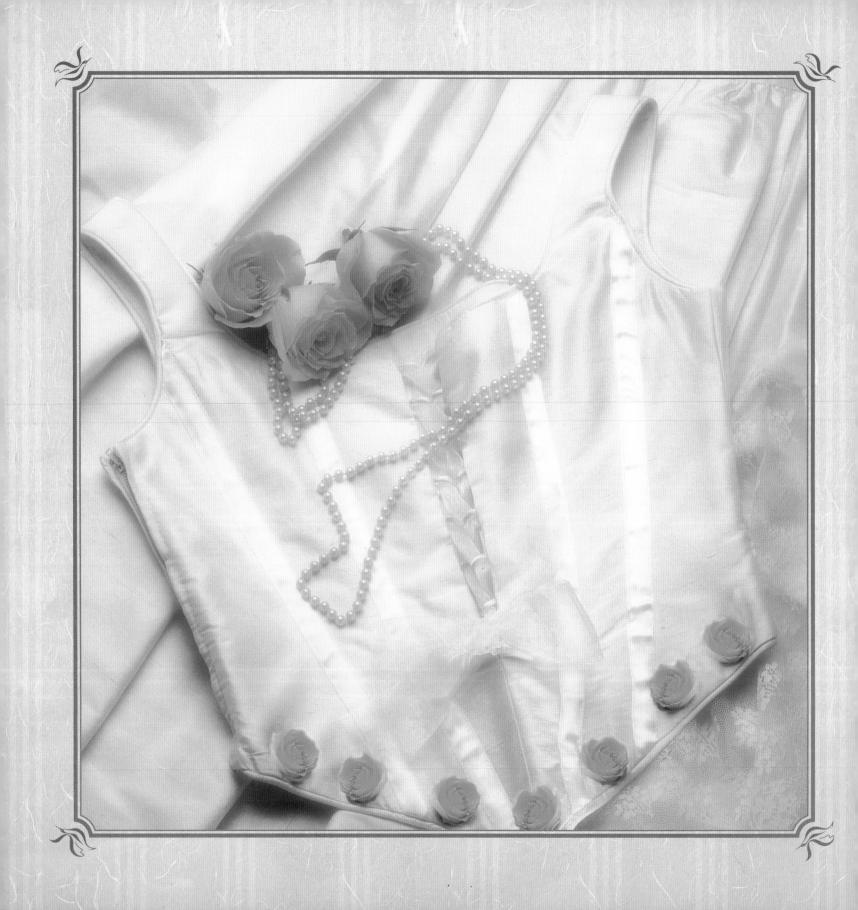

Here Comes The Bride

My full name is _____

My date of birth is _____

I remember growing up in _____

I went to school at _____

And I graduated from _____

_____

My favorite hobbies and interests are _____

_____

_____

_____

If I were to look into my future I would like to see _____

_____

_____

_____

_____

THE HANDSOME GROOM

My full name is _____

My date of birth is _____

I remember growing up in _____

I went to school at _____

And I graduated from _____

_____

My favorite hobbies and interests are _____

_____

_____

If I were to look into a crystal ball I would see _____

_____

_____

_____

_____

My Loving Family

My mother's full name is _____

My father's full name is _____

My sisters _____

_____

My brothers _____

_____

My grandmother on my mother's side _____

My grandfather on my mother's side _____

My grandmother on my father's side _____

My grandfather on my father's side _____

My aunts, uncles and cousins _____

_____

_____

_____

HIS LOVING FAMILY

My mother's full name is _____

My father's full name is _____

My sisters _____

_____

My brothers _____

_____

My grandmother on my mother's side _____

My grandfather on my mother's side _____

My grandmother on my father's side _____

My grandfather on my father's side _____

My aunts, uncles and cousins _____

_____

_____

_____

Our Guest List

Our Guest List

SHOWER & WEDDING INVITATIONS
Attach Invitations Here

Our Bridal Showers & Parties

I remember the most special bridal shower was given by _____

_____

Our guest list included these friends and family members _____

_____

_____

I remember some of our most treasured gifts were _____

_____

_____

_____

_____

Our friends helped us celebrate by _____

_____

_____

_____

_____

Planning Our Wedding

I remember the first things we planned were _____

_____

_____

_____

This was a special part of our wedding that we spent time planning _____

_____

_____

_____

Our favorite part of the wedding plan was this special event _____

_____

_____

_____

Planning Our Wedding

We remember many friends and family helping us with our wedding preparations.
We would especially like to thank _____

_____

_____

_____

We chose these colors for our wedding because _____

_____

The flowers and bouquets were special to us because _____

_____

_____

_____

_____

_____

_____

PHOTOGRAPH

OUR REHEARSAL DINNER

Our rehearsal dinner was on _____

at _____

This is a list of the special people who attended the dinner _____

_____

_____

_____

Some of the special things that happened at the dinner were _____

_____

_____

_____

The most memorable toast was given by _____

_____

_____

_____

Our Wedding Day

I remember on the morning of the wedding, we were all up and busy by _____
Looking back, the funniest last-minute preparations included _____

_____

_____

_____

We would like to thank these people for all of their love and support _____

_____

_____

_____

_____

_____

_____

_____

Our Preparation

We remember the special things we did to pamper ourselves _____

_____

_____

Some of our favorite things were _____

_____

_____

Our wedding party made the preparation special by _____

_____

_____

This is how we tried to relax and stay calm _____

_____

_____

_____

_____

_____

My Wedding Attire

My wedding dress was special to me because _____

_____

I remember my favorite thing about my dress was _____

_____

Some extra special garments that accompanied my dress were _____

_____

My shoes were special to me because _____

_____

I remember I chose certain jewelry and accessories because _____

_____

_____

My favorite flowers in my bouquet were _____

_____

_____

Something Old, Something New Something Borrowed, Something Blue

I remember _____ gave me something old. This was special to me because _____

_____

For something new, I remember I chose _____
because _____

_____

I remember borrowing _____ from _____
It was special because _____

_____

_____

_____ gave me something blue. It was special to me because

_____

_____

MAID OF HONOR & BRIDESMAIDS

We chose _____ to be our Maid of Honor because she is very special.

_____

_____

_____

_____

She wore _____

_____

We remember we chose these bridesmaids because _____

_____

The bridesmaids wore _____

_____

_____

_____

_____

The Best Man & Groomsmen

We chose _____ to be our Best Man because he is very special.

We chose him for these special reasons _____

_____

_____

_____

He wore this attire _____

_____

Our groomsmen were _____

_____

We remember we chose these special groomsmen because _____

_____

_____

The groomsmen wore _____

_____

_____

PHOTOGRAPH

PHOTOGRAPH

OUR PHOTOGRAPHER

We remember our photographer _____

because _____

_____

_____

_____

The most memorable pose we did for the photographer was _____

_____

_____

_____

_____

_____

_____

_____

_____

Our Wedding Ceremony

Our wedding began at _____

_____

We chose to be married at this location _____

_____

We remember _____ married us.

_____

We chose _____ for music because _____

_____

I remember our ceremony was very special to us because _____

_____

_____

_____

_____

_____

PHOTOGRAPH

PHOTOGRAPH

Our Wedding Reception

We held our reception at _____

_____

This place is special to us because _____

_____

We remember a few stories about the reception _____

_____

_____

_____

_____

_____

We chose _____ for our wedding favors because ____

_____

_____

Have Guests Write Here

The Chosen Menu

We remember some of our favorite dishes at the reception were _____
_____
_____
_____
_____
_____
_____

This is how we had the tables and centerpieces set up _____
_____
_____
_____
_____
_____

Some Reception Rituals

_____ made the most memorable toast at the reception.

_____

_____

We remember our first dance together was to this favorite song_____

_____

Our wedding cake was made by _____

Here is a description of the kind of cake that we chose _____

_____

_____

We remember a funny story about cutting the cake together_____

_____

_____

_____

PHOTOGRAPH

PHOTOGRAPH

Our First Night Together

Our Honeymoon

We remember our honeymoon took us away to _____

_____

_____

We had so much fun because we stayed _____

_____

Our favorite memory of some fun things that we did together are _____

_____

_____

_____

_____

_____

Gifts We Received

Given By

Gift

_____ | _____

_____ | _____

_____ | _____

_____ | _____

_____ | _____

_____ | _____

_____ | _____

_____ | _____

_____ | _____

_____ | _____

_____ | _____

_____ | _____

GIFTS WE RECEIVED

Given By

Gift

GIFTS WE RECEIVED

Given By   Gift

_____   _____

_____   _____

_____   _____

_____   _____

_____   _____

_____   _____

_____   _____

_____   _____

_____   _____

_____   _____

_____   _____

Available Record Books From Havoc

A Celebration of Memories	It's All About Me!
A Circle of Love	Memories of My Garden
Baby	Mom
College Life	Mothers & Daughters
Couples	Mother & Son
Family	My Pregnancy
Forever Friends	Our Honeymoon
Friendship	Our Wedding
Generations	School Days
Girlfriends	Sisters
Grandmother	Tying the Knot
Grandparents	Twins
Heart to Heart	Your First Five Years

www.havocpub.com